HOW THEY LIVED

A CELTIC FAMILY

LUCILLA WATSON

Illustrated by
John James

Wayland

How They Lived

An American Pioneer Family
A Celtic Family
A Child in Victorian London
A Colonial American Merchant
A Crusading Knight
An Edwardian Household
A Family in the Fifties
A Family in World War I
A Family in World War II
An Ice Age Hunter
An Inca Farmer
A Medieval Serf

A Plains Indian Warrior
A Plantation Slave
A Roman Centurion
A Samurai Warrior
A Saxon Farmer
A Slave in Ancient Greece
A Soldier in Wellington's Army
A Teenager in the Sixties
A Tudor Merchant
A Victorian Factory Worker
A Viking Sailor

Edited by Amanda Earl

First published in 1987 by
Wayland (Publishers) Limited
61 Western Road, Hove
East Sussex BN3 1JD, England

© Copyright 1987 Wayland (Publishers) Limited

British Library Cataloguing in Publication Data
Watson, Lucilla
A Celtic family. – (How they lived/Wayland)
1. Iron age – Great Britain – Juvenile
literature
I. Title   II. James, John, *1959–*   II. Series
936.1'004916   GN780.22.G7

ISBN 0 85078 803 X

Typeset by Kalligraphics Limited, Redhill, Surrey.
Printed and bound in Belgium by Casterman S.A.

CONTENTS

PREPARING FOR THE FEAST

There was a bustle in the hill-fort. Preparations for the feast had been going on for days, but now all the families were hurrying to complete their special tasks. Etain and her mother were preparing pigs for roasting. Using small iron knives, they gutted the carcasses and threw the hooves and guts into a pit nearby. Meanwhile, Etain's brother, Arawn, helped his father and uncle finish building a huge bonfire.

Carts pulled by oxen had brought vegetables from the surrounding farmsteads. Sheep and pigs had also been driven up to the hill-fort. Most would be slaughtered and roasted for the feast, but some were to be offered as sacrifices that night. Large barrels of freshly brewed beer were stacked outside the huts for the celebration.

Dusk was falling and soon the

4

festivities would begin. The families in the hill-fort were about to enjoy the feast of Lughnasa, celebrated in August each year. When the sacrifices and ceremonies had been performed and the gods thanked for another harvest safely gathered, there would be singing, dancing, eating and drinking.

Celtic civilization began in about 700BC, in a region just north of the Alps. As their civilization grew, the Celts spread throughout central and western Europe. The first Celts reached Britain in about 450BC. Britain at that time was in the Bronze Age. People made most of their tools and implements out of bronze.

The Celts brought with them important new knowledge – they knew how to make things out of iron. Iron, being much stronger than bronze, made better tools and weapons. So the Celts started the Iron Age in Britain, which lasted until AD43, when the Romans conquered Britain and destroyed the Celtic civilization.

The feast of Lughnasa was a time of great excitement to the Celts. Every member of the family was involved in preparing for the celebrations.

5

KINGS, TRIBES AND THE FAMILY

Celtic society was made up of many tribes, each ruled by its own king. Here we see a craftsman making tools for the other tribe members.

Everyone in Celtic society belonged to a tribe. Tribes were made up of many families, living as a community. There were over thirty tribes in Celtic Britain, each one ruled by its own king.

The king had a group of advisers to help him rule his tribe and protect it from attack by other tribes. The king's advisers were important noblemen and learned priests called druids. The druids were in charge of all Celtic religious ceremonies. They were experts at looking into the future. They advised the king on what the gods might be trying to tell him.

Below the druids in society came the warriors and their charioteers (chariot drivers). Warriors were important in Celtic society for they defended the tribe and stood for

This detail of the handle of the Aylesford bucket shows the skill of the Celtic craftsmen.

strength, heroism and valour – qualities which the Celts found important. Next, came the poets and musicians. The musicians sang songs and recited exciting stories to entertain the king and his advisers. Skilled craftsmen and land-owning farmers were next in importance.

Ordinary people in Celtic society were mostly simple craftsmen, or poor farm workers and servants. A craftsman, such as a blacksmith, would work at one of the furnaces in the hill-fort, making tools like sickles and knives and doing everyday repairs. Most Celtic families led a simple life with few luxuries and little excitement, but they lived in relative safety, the safety of the hill-fort.

This Celtic iron bucket was found at Aylesford in Kent.

7

SAFE IN THE HILL-FORT

Life in Celtic times was often dangerous. Tribes needed to protect themselves against attack from other tribes. One of the best ways to do this was to build a hill-fort. Hill-forts were fortified enclosures built on the top of a hill with a good view of the surrounding countryside. In the largest hill-forts, there was room for a whole tribe – the king, nobles, warriors, craftsmen, farmers and all their families. Farm animals, such as cattle, were also kept inside the hill-fort in times of danger, but they were mostly left to graze in the surrounding fields.

Smaller hill-forts only held a few families. In such small communities, there would be one king who ruled over several hill-forts.

Building a hill-fort was hard work. Teams of men began by digging a deep ditch round the top of the hill. As they worked, they flung the earth on to the ground above them. Gradually, this made a steep bank all round the hill, just above the ditch. The bank was made stronger and higher

by stakes being hammered into the ground to make a fence or palisade. An army trying to attack the hill-fort would be trapped in the ditch while soldiers defending it could shoot arrows and hurl stones from behind the palisade. The simplest hill-forts had just one ditch and bank. Others had three or even four, one inside the other, for extra safety.

The simplest entrances to hill-forts were wooden gates, built across an opening in the bank. Others had more complicated entrances, built almost like a maze. A system of narrow passages, with steep earth banks on each side, helped to confuse and trap the enemy.

Maiden Castle, Dorset. The remains of this hill-fort show how important safety was to the Celts.

To frighten the enemy, warriors painted their bodies with dyes.

A CELTIC FAMILY'S HOME

A typical scene of Celtic daily life. While the women and children weave and thresh corn, the men dig pits and thatch the roof of a hut.

Inside the ramparts, it was rather like a small village. Families lived together in groups of huts which were positioned to form small streets. The huts were round or rectangular, with a doorway on one side. They were made from sturdy wooden posts and wattle and daub walls. Making wattle and daub walls was just another everyday job for the men in the hill-fort. They began by weaving bendy branches together, probably working round the house, from post to post. Then they spread clay or mud on to the network of branches, to make a solid wall. The roof was made out of thatch or turf, and a hole was left in the centre to let smoke from the fire escape.

Inside a Celtic family's hut it was dark, and the air was usually filled with strong smells of cooking and burning wood. The women prepared gruel and made stews in an iron cauldron hanging from a chain over the hearth. There would be bowls and large storage jars on the ground, and straw or animal skins spread out for the family to sit or sleep on.

Some huts were used as storehouses for hay and other winter supplies. Grain was usually stored in pits dug in the ground. The pits were carefully sealed with clay to stop the grain going mouldy. Old, empty pits soon became rubbish tips for broken jars, bones and left-over food.

Hill-fort life was always busy. Women threshed grain, ground flour on querns, or wove cloth on upright looms. Children often helped the women with their weaving. Potters produced many bowls and jars to replace those that got broken. Blacksmiths worked at their furnaces, making farm tools or repairing harnesses. They also taught their sons the trade for the future. And there would always be new huts to build or thatch roofs to mend.

This was the daily life of a Celtic family in times of peace. But when rumours of a marauding tribe reached the hill-fort, watchmen would be positioned on the ramparts and families would grow nervous.

A typical example of a Celtic cooking cauldron, which would be hung over the fire.

LAKE VILLAGES

Not all Celtic families in Britain lived in hill-forts. In flat, marshy areas, they built lake villages. Lake villages were actually boggy islands built in the middle of a lake. The Celts made the bog stronger and dryer by adding a layer of logs, brushwood, stones and clay. To make their village safer, they built a palisade of stakes, filled in with wattle and daub, all round the edge of the island.

The lake-dwellers paddled to and from dry land in canoes. Inside the lake village, there were the same wattle and daub huts as in a hill-fort, and the same everyday activities, like potting, weaving, cooking and metal-working. Although life in a lake village was always slightly damp, one advantage was being able to catch fresh fish from the water.

Other families of Celts, particularly the larger ones, lived in strongholds known as *oppida*. These strongholds were usually built near marshland or rivers. The sides of the

stronghold not facing the river or marsh were defended by a system of dykes (steep banks of earth). It was impossible to drive war chariots over the dykes, so the stronghold was well protected.

In Scotland, some Celtic families lived in round stone towers, called *brochs*. Brochs had a ground floor and a first floor, linked by a stone stairway. Animals were kept on the ground floor and the families lived upstairs, for extra safety.

Celts in Scotland lived in brochs. *Old ruins of brochs can be found over much of Scotland today.*

Lake villages were better protected than hill-forts as they were surrounded by water.

CLOTHES AND APPEARANCE

The Celts were a tall, strong, fair-skinned people. They were very proud of their appearance, and made beautifully polished bronze mirrors in which to admire themselves. Celtic women wore their hair long, either loose or plaited. Celtic men often treated their hair with chalk to make it appear lighter and spikey. Most men shaved, but let their moustaches grow so long that it was difficult for them to eat or drink.

The Celts' appearance was very important to them. The men and women alike wore their hair long and wore brightly coloured woven clothes.

The Celts often used paints and make-up to decorate themselves. Warriors painted their bodies with woad, a blue dye, to make themselves look even more fearsome. Celtic women wore make-up made from berries and herbs to colour their cheeks and eyebrows. They also stained their fingernails with dye from vegetables.

A Celtic brooch – worn by rich or important Celts to fasten their cloaks.

A beautifully decorated Celtic mirror.

Celtic clothes were brightly coloured. The men wore tight trousers and tunics, the women wore loose woollen dresses and the children wore simple tunics. Both men and women wore cloaks – a thick weave in winter and a thin weave in summer. All clothes were woven in colourful stripes and tartan patterns. Shoes were made of leather, or linen and leather.

The Celts also loved jewellery. Women wore gold or bronze pins in their hair, and colourful glass beads round their necks. Rich or important Celts fastened their cloaks with a bronze brooch and wore heavy bronze bracelets and anklets. Gold torques were the most precious piece of jewellery, worn only by people of the highest rank. Poor people, however, wore less brightly coloured clothes and hardly any jewellery, apart from simple bone ornaments.

This gold necklace – known as a torque – was the most valued piece of jewellery to the Celts.

15

FARMING AND FOOD

In the countryside around the hill-forts, the Celts grew crops and raised animals. The open landscape was dotted with hamlets, farmsteads and patches of small, squarish fields. These fields, now called Celtic fields, were marked out by low, untidy walls made from the stones that plough-men threw aside as they tended the fields. Ploughing was done with a simple wooden plough, called an ard, pulled along by a pair of oxen.

The Celts grew turnips, cabbages, beans and parsnips. Their main crops were wheat and barley, which were stored for the winter. The grain was harvested with small iron or bronze sickles and stored in large jars, or in pits. Flour from the ground grain could be made into porridge, or added to soups to make them

A wooden ard *pulled by oxen was used for ploughing the land.*

thicker. Loaves of bread were baked on hot stones near the fire.

Celtic farmers kept pigs, cattle, sheep and goats. These animals provided fresh meat, as well as milk for making cheese. The Celts also enjoyed hunting wild animals like deer and boar.

For a typical Celtic meal, meat was roasted over the fire on an iron spit or wrapped in straw and baked in the hot embers. Stews were also made and left to bubble slowly in an

The interior of Celtic huts all looked much the same as this one. The quern (shown right) was an instrument used to grind flour.

iron cauldron. Meat that was not needed at once was salted, or hung up in the roof of the hut where it was quickly smoked by the fire. It was important to keep smoked and salted meats for the long, hungry winter months.

17

FAMILY LIFE

Above *Some Celtic pottery storage jars.*

Beautiful Iron Age silver cups.

Left *Mealtimes were of great importance to the Celts.*

Celtic family life was always busy. Inside the huts, women spun wool and wove cloth and made cooking pots out of clay. The women also prepared meals, baked bread and made cheese. Children and elderly members of the family helped with everyday chores.

Most men from ordinary families went about their special crafts, like carpentry, or worked in the fields, ploughing, harvesting or sowing. Young boys might be sent out to watch over grazing cattle.

The children of important families had a rather different life. Boys were fostered by other noble families, where they were taught how to become warriors. Rich girls were also brought up by foster families until they got married.

For rich and poor alike, mealtimes were an important part of Celtic family life. At mealtimes, families would crowd into their huts. They ate sitting on the floor, tearing pieces of meat with their hands and chewing on hunks of bread. There would also be a great deal of beer, which the Celts drank from pottery or wooden cups.

In a rich household there would be wine, an expensive luxury, imported from the Continent, drunk from dainty silver cups. When they had finished eating, the Celts loved to pass the evening with stories, songs and poems about the tribe or the brave deeds of mythical heroes. Although these stories were long, the musicians of the tribe knew them off by heart. As the children's beds were only a metre or so away, they could listen with the adults for as long as they could stay awake.

Iron, Bronze and Gold

Until the Celts arrived, no one in Britain knew how to smelt iron ore to make tools and weapons. The Celts smelted iron ore in clay furnaces filled with charcoal. Large leather bellows fanned the furnace, producing enough heat to purify the iron and make it soft enough to be beaten into shape. Celtic blacksmiths held the smoldering hot iron with a pair of long-handled tongs and beat it out with a hammer. As well as ordinary items like sickles and cauldrons, Celtic blacksmiths made spearheads, scabbards, swords, daggers and wheels for the warrior's chariots. Blacksmiths also beat lumps of red-hot iron into long,

This craftsman is making spearheads from iron, which was smelted in furnaces like the one behind him.

A terret (or bit) was attached to the harness-pad of a horse for driving-reins to pass through.

bronze could be melted down and poured into moulds. The finest sword hilts and shields were made in this way, often decorated with swirling patterns and set with brightly coloured enamel or coral.

Gold was the most precious metal. Only the richest men and women wore gold torques, which were heavy

sword-shaped ingots, which were used as a form of money.

Bronze was used mostly for jewellery and decoration on swords, shields and harnesses. Unlike iron,

A Celtic sword and sheath, made from bronze and iron.

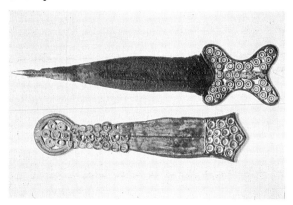

This bronze V-shaped helmet, found in the Thames, was used for ceremonial purposes.

necklaces made by twisting strands of gold together. Each end of the torque was finished with a heavy ring, called a terminal.

RELIGION AND RITUAL

Religion was very important to the Celts. Everyone, from the richest to the poorest families, respected the gods.

The Celts thought of their gods as strong, clever, superhumans. Every tribe had its own god. The tribal god kept law and order in the tribe and helped fend off disease. Celtic goddesses (the wives of the gods) were thought to look after the new crops and young animals in the fields.

Some hill-forts had a religious temple where the druids conducted their ceremonies. Rituals were also performed in sacred places beside a lake or river, for the Celts believed mysterious spirits lived there. To show the tribe's respect, the druids would throw fine swords and shields into the water as gifts to the gods.

Some woodland areas were also considered to be holy places, for spirits were thought to live among

This shield, thrown into the water as an offering to the gods, was found in the River Thames at Battersea.

A detail from the red 'enamel' and bronze roundel at the centre of the Battersea shield.

Beautifully decorated swords and shields were thrown into the nearest river or lake by druids, as gifts to the gods.

the trees. For this reason, the oak tree was sacred and mistletoe was valued for its strange power to heal wounds and cure diseases.

At a special altar in the temple or in a forest clearing living sacrifices were offered to the gods. When the animal (usually a bull or calf) had been killed, the druids would peer into the animal's insides hoping to make out a message from the gods.

The most gruesome ritual was the human sacrifice. Groups of people were chained together and thrown into a lake, or pushed into a deep pit where they fell on sharp stakes.

23

FESTIVALS AND CELEBRATIONS

As part of their religious ceremonies, the Celts held large feasts or festivals. There were four important religious festivals in the Celtic year.

A Celtic family began celebrating the new year on the eve of 1 November, with the terrifying feast of Samain. This was a night of great danger, when the spirits of the Otherworld were let loose and supernatural forces made strange things happen. Sacrifices would be offered up to the ghosts and spirits of the Otherworld.

The second feast of the Celtic year was the feast of Imbolc, celebrated

on 1 February. This feast was devoted to Brigid, the goddess of sheep and all farm animals. By offering sacrifices and performing rites in her honour, the Celts believed that Brigid would make sure that lambs would be born in the spring and that the ewes would have enough milk to feed them.

Beltane was the third feast, celebrated on 1 May. The magical rites performed at Beltane encouraged crops to grow and farm animals to stay healthy. Druids lit large bonfires and drove herds of farm animals through the smoke and flames. By doing this, the Celts believed that their cattle had been cleansed.

The last feast in the Celtic year was Lughnasa, named after King Lughnasa, the king of harvest festival. Although the feast itself was held on 1 August, the festivities and rites went on for a whole month. The Celts praised their gods for good crops safely harvested and healthy cattle.

At the feast of Beltane, Celts would force their animals to walk through fire, as they believed that this would cleanse them of evil.

THE TRIBE IN DANGER

The Celts loved action and excitement. One Roman historian remarked that they were 'madly fond of war'. It was usually only the sons of the higher-ranking Celtic families who became the tribe's most respected warriors. But when the tribe was in danger, all able-bodied men were expected to fight.

The aim of the Celtic army was to look as frightening as possible and make as much noise as they could. Foot soldiers went into battle shouting, banging on their shields and

blowing on their long horns to terrify the enemy.

Celtic warriors made themselves look startling by painting their bodies with woad. They wore no armour and hardly any clothes, and most were too proud of their hair to cover it with a helmet. For weapons, they mainly used a sword, a sling, spears, and a wooden or bronze shield.

Warriors went into battle in small, wooden chariots pulled by a pair of ponies. In each chariot stood a warrior and his charioteer. The charioteer would force ponies to run as fast as they could towards the enemy. The warrior in the back would hurl his spears at the enemy, then jump down and fight with his sword. Meanwhile, the charioteer stood ready and waiting to whisk the warrior away to safety.

Celtic battles were chaotic. Sometimes they were just displays of strength and bravery. But after real battles, thc Celts kept the heads of enemies that they had killed. They treated these heads as sacred objects and displayed them in their temples.

A warrior and charioteer leave the hill-fort to go into battle.

27

A Celtic Burial

The Celts believed in life after death. They thought that when people died they went to a place called the Otherworld. Everyone went to the Otherworld, whether they had been good or bad in their real lives. The Otherworld was a happy place. All the Celtic gods lived there too.

The Celts sent their dead to the Otherworld in two different ways. When a Celt died, the body could be burnt and the bones placed in a pottery jar, or the body could be laid in a grave and covered by a barrow. The bodies or burnt remains of important people were buried with all kinds of luxuries. Jewellery and precious objects were placed in the grave, and there would also be joints

Poor Celts were buried in a simple grave.

Objects like these, found in the remains of a Celtic tomb, were buried with rich Celts to help them in the Otherworld.

of meat, a cauldron for cooking, jars of wine and fine silver cups.

Warriors were buried with their swords, shields and spears, and sometimes with their chariots. Even horses were buried with some warriors.

Only kings, noblemen and warriors were given rich burials. Ordinary people went on their journey to the Otherworld with only a simple piece of jewellery or a single joint of meat. The poorest went with nothing at all.

THE DESTRUCTION OF THE CELTS

The world of the Celts in Britain came to a sudden end. By AD43, the Romans, having conquered France, were ready to cross the Channel to Britain. They knew that Britain was inhabited by fierce Celts, but had also heard that it was a rich land.

Julius Caesar tried twice to land his army in Britain, but both times his army was driven back into their boats by the Celts. But under the leadership of Claudius, the Romans succeeded in beating the Celts. Soon the Romans established themselves in Britain. They built towns and roads and kept the Celts under control with their large, organized armies. The Romans hunted down and killed the druids, who frightened them with their strange powers. Slowly, the Romans took over Britain, and the Celtic world faded away.

The Celtic language, some long Celtic poems and stories, the feast of Hallowe'en and the custom of picking mistletoe at Christmas are just a few traces of Celtic civilization that survive today.

Hadrian's Wall: a reminder of the Roman invasion of Britain which led to the destruction of Celtic civilization.

GLOSSARY

Anklet An ornament for the ankle.

Barrow A mound of earth built over a tomb.

Bellows A device for blowing air into a fire to increase the flame.

Cauldron A large metal cooking pot.

Charcoal The black remains of partly burnt wood.

Civilization The development of a community or country.

Community A group of people living together in one place.

Dyke A steep bank of earth built as a defence.

Enclosure An area of land closed-in and secure.

Fortified Strengthened against attack.

Foster To look after a child for a period of time.

Furnace An enclosed chamber where metal is heated up to soften it.

Ingot A lump of metal, usually beaten into an oblong shape.

Iron ore Iron found in its natural state, mined with other substances.

Hearth The place where a fire is made.

Maraud To wander from place to place looting and raiding.

Mythical Something which is not based on fact, but on past legend.

Palisade A fence made of wooden stakes, usually for defensive purposes.

Quern A flat stone for grinding grain by hand with a smaller stone.

Ramparts The defences surrounding a hill-fort.

Rite A religious ceremony or prayer to a god.

Sacrifice Something offered to a god to show respect and honour.

Scabbard A case for a sword.

Sickle A sharp tool for harvesting crops, with a metal blade and a wooden handle.

Smelt To separate pure iron from iron ore, by heating it in a furnace.

Thresh To separate grain from the husks by sieving or beating the newly harvested crop.

Torque A large necklace of twisted metal.

Woad A deep blue dye made from the leaves of a special plant.

MORE BOOKS TO READ

Dyer, James, *Hillforts of England and Wales* (Shire Archaeology, 1981)

Quennell, C. B. H. and M., *Everyday Life in Prehistoric Times* (Batsford, 1973)

Stead, I. M., *Celtic Art* (British Museum, 1985)

Watson, Lucilla, *Boudicca and the Ancient Britons* (Wayland, 1986)

Place, Robin *The Celts* (Macdonald, 1977)

Sauvain, Philip *Before 1066 (History of Britain)* (Macmillan Educational, 1982)

INDEX

Picture acknowledgements
The pictures in this book were supplied by the following: Aerofilms 9 (top); The British Museum 7 (both), 15 (all), 19 (right), 21 (all), 22 (both), 29; The Colchester and Essex Museum 11, 19 (left); The Highlands and Islands development Board 13 (top); Topham Picture Library 30.